SCHLESWIG-HOLSTEIN
Land between sky and sea

Wachholtz Verlag

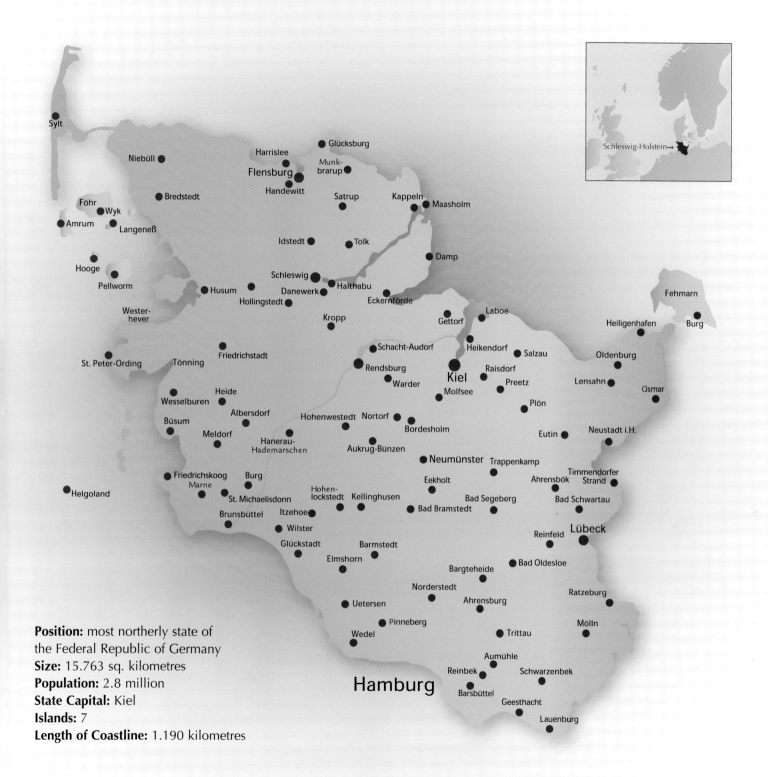

Schleswig-Holstein→

Sylt

Niebüll

Harrislee
Glücksburg
Munk-
brarup
Flensburg
Handewitt
Satrup
Kappeln
Maasholm

Föhr
Wyk
Bredstedt
Amrum
Langeneß
Idstedt
Tolk
Damp

Hooge
Pellworm
Schleswig
Haithabu
Husum
Danewerk
Hollingstedt
Eckernförde
Gettorf
Laboe
Fehmarn

Wester-
hever
Kropp
Burg
Heiligenhafen

St. Peter-Ording
Friedrichstadt
Schacht-Audorf
Heikendorf
Salzau
Oldenburg

Tönning
Rendsburg
Raisdorf
Lensahn
Gsmar

Heide
Warder
Kiel
Preetz

Wesselburen
Molfsee
Plön

Büsum
Albersdorf
Hohenwestedt
Nortorf
Bordesholm
Eutin
Neustadt i.H.

Meldorf
Hanerau-
Hademarschen
Aukrug-Bünzen
Neumünster
Trappenkamp

Helgoland
Friedrichskoog
Marne
Burg
Eekholt
Ahrensbök
Timmendorfer
Strand

St. Michaelisdonn
Hohen-
lockstedt
Kellinghusen
Bad Segeberg
Bad Schwartau

Brunsbüttel
Itzehoe
Bad Bramstedt
Reinfeld
Lübeck

Wilster

Glückstadt
Barmstedt

Elmshorn
Bargteheide
Bad Oldesloe
Ratzeburg

Norderstedt
Mölln

Uetersen
Ahrensburg

Pinneberg
Trittau

Wedel
Aumühle

Reinbek
Schwarzenbek

Hamburg
Barsbüttel
Geesthacht
Lauenburg

Position: most northerly state of
the Federal Republic of Germany
Size: 15.763 sq. kilometres
Population: 2.8 million
State Capital: Kiel
Islands: 7
Length of Coastline: 1.190 kilometres

Foreword

Schleswig-Holstein

Schleswig-Holstein is the most northerly state of the German Federal Republic. Its borders to the east and west are formed by the Baltic and the North Sea and to the south by the river Elbe, altogether conveying the impression of a geographical landmass completely intact within natural borders. Only to the north, after the plebiscite in 1920, was the border with Denmark finally and permanently defined. Homogenous and intact as Schleswig-Holstein appears on the map, there are nevertheless marked obvious geographical differences within this region. The natural, contrasting features consisting of marshland, sandy moorland and undulating moraine landscape are particularly characteristic, as are the low-lying North Sea coastal shore areas with their offshore and mudflats, large and tiny islands (Halligen) as well as the Baltic coast with its cliffs and sharply indenting fjords cutting deeply into the land.

Its geographical position has greatly influenced the varied history of this region and its development as a land bridge between central and northern Europe. This has facilitated the migration of peoples and cultural exchanges with central Europe and Scandinavia as well as foreign trade. To overcome the land barrier in the early days, use was made of waterways, which together with short land routes, connected both seas.

On the Baltic coast especially, important trade centres came into being to serve the trade with the Baltic states. The Hanseatic city of Lübeck even today is of considerable importance as a centre of commerce.

A considerable flow of goods is still transported via the Kiel Canal, one of the world's most important waterways.

Today, approximately 2.8 million people live in Schleswig-Holstein which has only two major cities: Kiel, the state capital and Lübeck, the old Hanseatic port.

Fishing and agriculture are the oldest branches of industry, threequarters of the total land area is still used for agriculture. The economic structure of Schleswig-Holstein is, however, broadly based. There are for instance more people employed in the computer industry than in agriculture. For many firms involved in the service and manufacturing industries it has become an attractive location. Tourism has had a long tradition and plays a vital role in this region. The seaside resorts on the North Sea and Baltic coasts are an annual attraction for many holidaymakers. The interior, too has much to offer the visitor. The three-part geological division of Schleswig-Holstein, i.e. the fertile hill country in the east with its many lakes, the central area with its sandy moorlands and infertile soil, the western area with its fertile marshland of silt deposited by the sea, often endangered by high tides, and its offshore islands and islets (Halligen), form the basis in this order for our journey in pictures throughout this region including its cities and towns.

Mölln is a lovingly cared-for small town dominated by the high hill on which stands the church of St. Nicholas. As early as the 13th century it provided an attractive stop on the much traversed saltroad from Lüneburg to Lübeck. Fortunately, the medieval character of the town centre still exists. On the high retaining wall of the churchyard can be seen the statue of Till Eulenspiegel, world-famous jester and symbol of the town, who according to legend died here sometime after the year 1350.

Ratzeburg in its attractive island setting, surrounded by the Nature Park Lauenburgische Seen is a rowing and fishing sports centre as well as a magnet for many visitors. The historical centre is surrounded by four lakes, and its 12th century Norman cathedral built by Henry the Lion is one of the most notable red-brick monumental edifices in Schleswig-Holstein. The artist Ernst Barlach, who lived in Ratzeburg, created the sculpture "The Beggar", seen in the cloister yard.

The decisive and influencing factor in the development of Bad Oldesloe was its function as a centre of commerce on the transit trade route Lübeck - Hamburg, together with salt-mining at a later stage. The town centre is dominated by the medieval old quarter surrounded by the rivers Trave and Beste. Old and modern architecture near the Stadthaus forms an attractive contrast.

The well-known landmark of the district town Bad Segeberg is the Kalkberg which well into the 17th century was surmounted by a dominating castle. During the following centuries the inhabitants of the town reduced the height of the castle rock by at least 20 metres by selling the chalk as a much-desired building material. Today it measures only 90 metres in height. What remains of the rock serves as a backdrop to the open air theatre for annually up to 300.000 visitors, who in summer come to see the popular Karl May Festival. Impressive insights into the fascinating world of bats can be gained by visiting the chalk caves and the adventure exhibition "Noctalis". The historical centre of the town is as much an attraction as the charming surrounding recreational area.

Lübeck, the famous Hanseatic city, founded in 1143, largely because of its convenient position soon became one of the most important and prosperous centres of trade with footholds in the whole of the Baltic region.
Its dignified townscape has been preserved for posterity and the old town centre, enclosed by water, with its roughly 1800 protected edifices was designated a world cultural heritage by the UNESCO in 1987. The Holstentor, part of the original fortified wall, is indeed the most famous attraction of the city, however only one among many, for Lübeck is regarded as the cultural capital of the north. Around the city varied and productive industries have been established with a special focus on medical equipment. The locally produced marzipan is of world-wide fame.

Lübeck was the home town of Thomas Mann who in his novel "Buddenbrooks" paints a vivid picture of the patrician way of life in which he grew up. The house in which many of the events described in the novel took place, has been preseved as a museum and can be visited.

One has only to stroll through the streets of Lübeck to sense the pervading atmosphere of the Hanseatic League. The Holy Ghost – Hospice is among the oldest social facilities in Europe. At the same time it is one of the most eminent monumental edifices of the Middle Ages.

Travemünde, one of the oldest seaside resorts, still attracts visitors with its chic and modern ambience. Here, maritime past and present meet attractively. The former training ship "Passat", Germany's last tall windjammer, can be visited on the Priwall.

Since the advent of the steamship the port of Travemünde has become an important point of departure for the ferry traffic to presently 25 partner towns along the Baltic Sea. It has become the biggest ferry harbour in Europe. For many years the old lighthouse has been out of use. Its function has now been taken over by the much taller Maritim-Hotel, from where light signals are transmitted to guide shipping.

Neustadt, an old fishing and harbour town, has a large square market-place
in the centre, preserved as part of its original layout. A pagoda-shaped storehouse,
built in 1828 close to the harbour bridge, has since then served as a grain
warehouse. In the summer the harbour presents a colourful scene with its moored
fishing boats and leisure sailing craft. A recently extended yacht harbour
and a specially reserved beach for surfers helped Neustadt's development towards
a centre of water sports in the area of Lübeck.

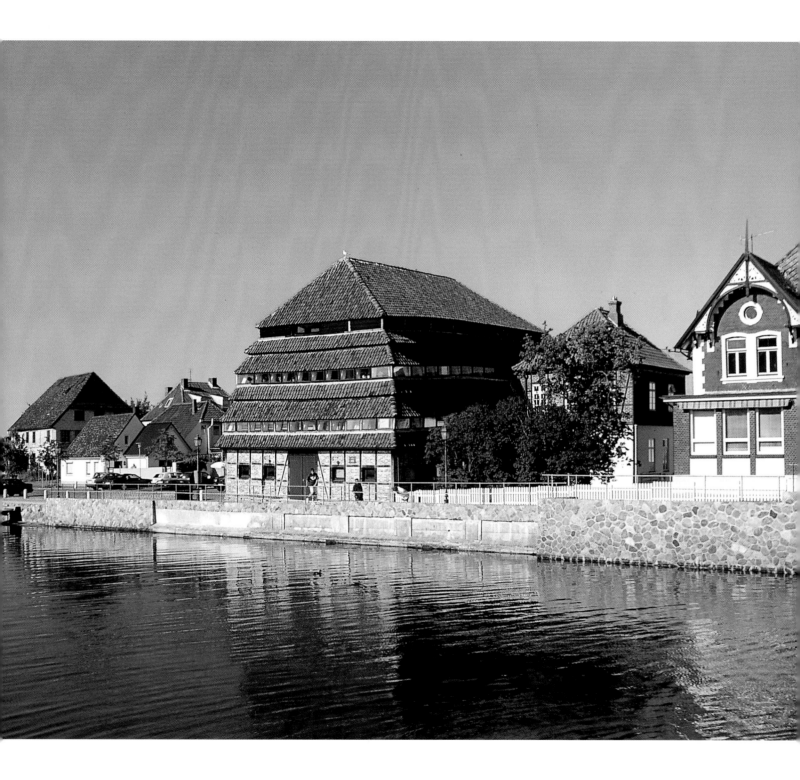

The "Schleswig-Holstein Music Festival", founded in 1986, is now of international cultural significance. The wide range of concerts and the annually changing focus on one particular nation allow concertgoers to get in touch with the many different facets offered by these nations.

Well-known and young up-and-coming musicians from all over the world perform not only in concert halls, but also in churches, manor houses, castles, riding halls and barns, all adding a special charm to the events.

During the summer months the cultural scene in Schleswig-Holstein is of special importance. Thousands of concertgoers are attracted to the musical events in rural surroundings as shown here on the Hasselburg estate.

In 1962 with the construction of a bridge across the Fehmarn Sound the island of Fehmarn was finally linked to the mainland. The "Vogelfluglinie" (direct line) providing a traffic link to Scandinavia has greatly affected the island's importance. The further link-up with Scandinavia is at the moment still done by ferries, but plans for a long bridge across the Belt are gradually materializing.

Fehmarn, the largest island in Schleswig-Holstein, has a rich and varied coastline. Blessed with an advantageous climate, the island boasts more than the average number of sunshine hours and less rainfall than is usual in the Federal Republic, an incentive for holidaymakers to come here earlier in the season. The island has remained an attractive recreational holiday destination.

Eutin, former prince-bishop's residence, is a picturesque, charming old town, set amidst a lovely lake landscape and surrounded by one of the most beautiful nature parks in Schleswig-Holstein, making it an attractive destination for many visitors. A stroll across the market square, through the town with its beautifully restored old houses of character and famed for its roses, is a pleasure at all times. The town reached its cultural peak at the end of the 18th century. Today, however, the people of Eutin do much to preserve the historical and cultural heritage of the past.

The baroque castle and its grounds laid out in the style of an English landscape garden are also focal points of interest and attraction. The summer performances of works by Carl Maria von Weber in the open air theatre adjacent to the lake are an added attraction here.

Horse breeding is a tradition in the Holsteinische Schweiz. The various breeds
resulting from these stud farms have gained recognition in the national
and international field of equestrian sports. Holstein cattle too, have achieved
their own world-wide fame.

The Holsteinische Schweiz presents an environment of peace and relaxation. The season of the flowering rape fields viewed against a background of a typical Schleswig-Holstein sky is a panorama of outstanding natural beauty.

On a fine day, from the observation tower Hessenstein, close to the Panker estate, one can see as far as the Danish islands.

Many of the region's stately homes are to be found in the Plön area. They were once the centre of aristocratic courtly life. With their enormous barns and stables they number amongst the large estates of the region. Their present owners endeavour to maintain the heritage of the once renowned way of life of the nobility in Schleswig-Holstein. The Panker estate is an excellent example of this.

The health resort of Plön is situated in the heart of the Holsteinische Schweiz on
the edge of the large lake. As a holiday centre Plön offers many opportunities
for both walking and water sports.
Plön Castle is the landmark of the town. This 17th century edifice, built in
three wings, served during the reign of the emperors as a school for officer cadets.
After recent extensive renovation it is now used as a training centre for the
Fiel-mann Academy (an international optical concern), an imposing sight when
viewed from one of the pleasure boats during a popular lake trip.

Laboe is situated at the mouth of the Kieler Förde. Standing high above this Baltic resort is the naval memorial in the shape of a ship's stern-post. Those who climb the 85 m high observation platform have a wonderful view over land and sea. The harbour of Laboe is the finishing post of the annual oldtimer regatta, when many of the most beautiful sailing yachts arrive and are to be seen.

The town centre, dominated by the tower of the town hall, together with its
pedestrian shopping precincts and a wide range of retail shops has become
a popular shopping venue, both for residents of the surrounding areas as well
as for the numerous Scandinavian tourists.

Kiel, the state capital, is situated on both banks of the inner Förde. The typical maritime aspect of Kiel with its harbour facilities, the enormous passenger ferries and portal cranes can be seen and felt everywhere. A university town since 1665, it later developed into a naval base and has since grown from a small medieval town to a large city with a naval and shipyard presence. The November Revolution in 1918 was set in motion by sailors of the warships stationed in Kiel. After World War II extensive rebuilding of the town was necessary as a result of the large areas of the city destroyed during air raids.

The state government building is situated directly alongside the Förde. It is the home of the Schleswig-Holstein state government and state parliament. A red light on the art-object in front of the glass extension indicates that Parliament is in session. It is also the start of the beautiful Förde promenade called the "Kiellinie", an attraction during the "Kieler Woche" for thousands of visitors.

The "Kieler Woche" with its 125- year-old tradition is one of the world's largest sailing sports events, well-known outside Schleswig-Holstein. Twenty-two classes of boats compete in regatta events that take place in the Kieler Förde. This event is accompanied by a magnificent city-festival with diverse cultural and light entertainment highlights.

The Kiel Canal was officially opened in 1895 and ranks as one of the most used man-made waterways in the world. The especially large locks in Kiel-Holtenau enable ships of up to 9.5 m draught to enter the canal and so avoid the roundabout route through the Great Belt near Denmark.

During the 14th and 15th centuries according to legend pirate ships set off from Eckernförde. Now people head for the fish market in the harbour to buy herring, cod, and flounder. Fish processing, too, is an established tradition in the town, and the famous "Kieler Sprotte" has its origin here. A stroll through the inviting pedestrian precinct leads one inevitably to the attractive harbour. The opposite side of the harbour is reached via a wooden bridge. Constructed in 1872 by pioneers during a flood, it is still very much in use today.

For hundreds of years Damp was a sleepy little village. All this changed when in the seventies the holiday centre "Damp 2000" was built. This holiday centre, largely traffic-free, offers relaxation not only to the holidaymakers but – due to innovative and integrated medical care - also to patients of the Rehabilitation/Baltic Sea Clinic.

Haithabu was once the most important settlement in Europe and at the same time medieval trading place on the Baltic. After its destruction it became the site of Schleswig-Holstein's oldest town, Schleswig, founded on the northbank of the river Schlei. St. Peter's Cathedral, one of the most impressive historical monuments here, is indicative of the importance of this town. Schloss Gottorf, the largest castle in Schleswig-Holstein, is to be found on the outskirts of Schleswig. A splendid complex of the Renaissance period, it houses the state's museums. Unique exhibitions ranging from notable pre-historic finds to contemporary art are a regular feature here.

The period of the Vikings is brought to life in the Museum of Haithabu, situated right next to the original medieval town, where amongst other items a thousand-year old ship and reconstructions of medieval edifices can be seen.

The fishing communities on the Schlei impart an idyllic charm. Holm in Schleswig and Arnis, the smallest town in Germany, have retained their original character. Today in Kappeln, fish is still caught using the old medieval method of herring fences.

Rum has long been the basis of Flensburg's fame and fortune. At the end of the 18th century Flensburg's merchants received the raw cane sugar for the making of rum from the West Indies. Up to the present day the tradition of making spirits and beer has continued. Flensburg is the most northerly town of Germany. It has a tradition of 700 years as a trading and harbour town, and lies nestled alongside the 34 kilometres long Flensburg fjord.

Formerly the largest Danish trading town, Flensburg now plays an important role as a border commercial centre. The town itself and its beautiful surrounding countryside is an attraction for many visitors. The "Alexandra", built in 1908, is the last remaining seagoing passenger steamship in Germany.

The castle of Glücksburg, not far from the Flensburger Förde, belongs among the principal works of Renaissance building. It was formerly a ducal residence and later in the 19th century the seat of the kings of Denmark. It is considered the cradle of European royalty. Close to the castle, on the premises of the former castle nursery, the rosarium Glücksburg can be admired which was founded in 1991 by the rose expert Ingwer J. Jensen.

Rendsburg, largely because of its central position, is the focal point of this region. The Paradeplatz is the centre of the town, in its immediate vicinity the most beautiful restored buildings can be seen, one of which is the Arsenal. Old and new houses together create a harmonious impression within the town.

The construction of a canal in the 18th century created the link between Rendsburg and Kiel. The building of the Kiel Canal provided Rendsburg with the necessary traffic network for its industrial development, especially shipbuilding. A landmark of the town is the rail bridge which, as a unique feature, functions together with a hover ferry.

Neumünster's trade and commerce since its founding have been favourably influenced because of its central position. Its leather and textile industries have made it famous well beyond its borders. A new museum helps to keep this period alive. In the sixties new industries were encouraged to establish themselves as a counterbalance to the declining traditional industries. Today Neumünster is still an important centre of commerce, a location for trade fairs and an equestrian stronghold with a long tradition. In the middle of the town is the Grossflecken, the market and commercial hub of this thriving area.

The river Schwale flows through Neumünster. The green areas adjacent to the banks of the river, together with the pond in the center of the town are popular meeting places. Well worth a visit, during a stroll through the town, is the Vicelin church, completed in 1834, a notable example of the north German classical period.

The Ständehaus in Itzehoe, built in the late classical style, is recognised as the birthplace of the parliamentary system of Schleswig-Holstein. The building is still used for meetings of the town council. It is situated next to the historical town hall, erected at the end of the 17th century. The idyllic atmosphere of the town centre is dominated by the tower of the Laurentii church. Tradition and progress exist here side by side. Evidence of this is the "Frauenhofer-Institut für Siliziumtechnologie" (ISiT) close to the IZET, a centre of innovation and since 1997 a technology and foundation centre.

For 200 years, Glückstadt on the river Elbe was the home port of the whaling ships that sailed the polar seas. The town became an important trading place for agricultural produce due to the surrounding fertile marshland soil.
In addition to the original "Glückstadt Matjes" herring the town also boasts many enchanting period houses.

Heide, the administrative seat of the district of Dithmarschen, is proud of its spacious market place. With an area of 4.7 hectares it is the largest in the Federal Republic. It also served as a place of assembly during the medieval peasants` republic. 48 regents assembled here every Saturday, passed laws, administered justice and punishments. Since that time the traditional weekly market has been held here on Saturdays. The St. Jürgen church in its present form has stood on this square since the 17th century.

Traces of early settlements in Schleswig-Holstein are to be found in many places. Besides the two megalithic graves in the vicinity of Albersdorf an Schwabstedt, a further 300 have been preserved. In these "Hünenbetten", put up 2000 years before Christ, presumably whole clans of the upper social strata were buried. Large boulders positioned in a circle covered with stone slabs were then piled with earth in the shape of mounds. With the passage of time, rain and wind have swept away the earth, leaving the megalithic stones exposed as monuments.

From time immemorial the everchanging drama of the tides has held the people of the west coast in awe. However, since 1973, the Eider Dam has provided protection against damage for land and population. The five individual gates prevent the penetration of the North Sea during a flood. At low tide the gates are opened allowing the collected water to flow back into the river Eider.

The prawn boats still provide a picturesque scene at Büsum's harbour and are an attraction for many of the holidaymakers visiting the seaside resort.

In the coastal regions the salt meadows of the temporarily flooded shore areas provide an important habitat for approximately 2000 species of animal and plant life. The manor house at Hoyerswort with its attached barn was once the seat of the governor of Eiderstedt. The barn has the typical features of an early farmhouse. These farm-buildings, then normally used as living quarters, are impressive because of their enormous size.

A unique attraction on the sandbank outside St. Peter-Ording are the houses on stilts. Protected from flooding, they provide facilities for the many holiday-makers using the wide stretch of the beach. Even in winter this resort retains its charm and is an attraction for many walkers.

Friedrichstadt is a preserved architectural jewel. Walking along the tree-lined "Grachten" one can easily imagine oneself in a small Dutch town, not without reason, for this town was originally built by Dutch religious refugees and has always been a sanctuary for many different religious communities.

Husum will retain for all time the description that its most famous son
Theodor Storm (1817-1888) wrote about it, hence the reputation "the grey
town by the sea". However, when in spring thousands of crocusses flower
in the castle grounds, this unfair description no longer continues to be true.

Around the market place many fine buildings are to be seen, relics from Husum's heyday as an important port. In contrast to these period houses stands the modern town hall situated directly on the harbour which architecturally resembles a boathouse.

The everchanging mood of the landscape created by the elements of wind and water was a constant inspiration to the expressionist painter Emil Nolde (1867-1956). His colourful and distinctive landscape paintings are evidence of this. His house in Seebüll is now a museum. Many of his flower paintings were painted in his own garden.

Since 1634, Amrum's sailors have sailed as crew members on Dutch whaling ships into the Arctic Sea, often as captains and helmsmen, which can be verified from their handsome tombstones. After whaling was no longer profitable, many of these mariners emigrated to America to seek their fortune. Most of the thatched Friesian-style houses have become sought-after accommodation for holidaymakers. Amrum's lighthouse is the highest on the North Sea coast and with a range of 40 kms is an important guide for shipping.

Wyk on the island of Föhr is the oldest seaside resort on the west coast. As early as 1819, the inhabitants of Föhr realised that there were other sources of income apart from seafaring. The island can be reached with ferries of the Wyker Dampfschiffs-Reederei. Föhr is quite rightly known as the "Green Island".

In 1927 the Hindenburg Causeway linking Sylt to the mainland was built.
The island is famous for its unique and beautiful coastline. It is hard to imagine
when enjoying such a tranquil end-of-the-day atmosphere on the beach that
it can be the scene of storms with waves from the North Sea up to 17 metres high
pounding that same beach and again and again wearing away the coastline.

In Sylt's capital, the exclusive seaside resort of Westerland, one almost has the feeling of being in urban surroundings. In contrast to which are situated the charming, preserved places on the island where the Friesian-style of building is very much maintained. A good example is Wenningstedt, where the door of a house belonging to a whaler would bear witness to the prosperity of the owner.

Helgoland is the only German island on the open sea, dramatic with its unmistakeable red rock standing out of the dark waters. The tall rock called "Lange Anna", almost 50 metres high, is the landmark of the island. The traffic-free island with an area of less than 1 square kilometre almost met its end when in April 1947 6,000 tons of ammunition were exploded. Since then Helgoland has once again become a popular destination for both holiday-makers and day-trippers, largely because of its healthy sea air and duty-free privileges. As a port of refuge and shelter, Helgoland is an important maritime resort in the North Sea.

Imprint

Photos:

Uwe Paulsen, Peter Schuster, Günther Meisterling, Manfred Finke,
H. Dietrich Habbe, Sönke Dwenger, Rosarium Glücksburg, Schöning Media,
Ostseeklinik Damp GmbH, Archäologisches Landesmuseum, Schloss Gottorf

Translation: Günter Schubert

Schleswig-Holstein - Land between sky and sea
is available in the following languages:

German   ISBN 978 3 529 05337 5
English   ISBN 978 3 529 05338 2
French   ISBN 978 3 529 05339 9
Low German   ISBN 978 3 529 05340 5
Danish   ISBN 978 3 529 05341 2
Spanish   ISBN 978 3 529 05342 9

© 2007 by Wachholtz Verlag, Neumünster